# INVESTING FOR YOUNG ADULTS

How to Earn, Save, Invest,
Grow Your Money, and Retire Early!

**Kris Pearson**

ISBN: 978-1-957590-32-5

For questions, email: Support@AwesomeReads.org

**Please consider writing a review!**

Just visit: AwesomeReads.org/review

# FREE BONUS

## SCAN TO GET OUR NEXT BOOK FOR FREE!

# TABLE OF CONTENTS

## Chapter Eight: Understanding Credit and Avoiding Debt Traps........................................... 88

## Chapter Nine: Make Smart & Lucrative Investments........................................................... 97

# INTRODUCTION

Many people dream of being financially independent. Financial independence is what really enables you to take charge of the course of your life, and to make and act on your own decisions. If you have achieved true financial independence, you may be less likely to need to ask permission before taking a risk or making a change; you are the one in charge of your money and how you spend it.

There are many ways to achieve financial independence over time, and it really does take time. You may slowly and steadily build a career or hone a craft that brings you an income; by saving that income carefully and spending it wisely, you can ensure your financial independence over the course of your early adulthood. In addition, making sound investments can eventually lead to your financial independence.

*Investment* refers to dedicating some of your money in a way that, with luck and some skill, will allow it to grow over time. There are many types of investments that people make. They invest in stocks or bonds that they hope will pay strong *dividends*; that is, the income

2

that investments pay to their shareholders based on their profits. Others might invest in start-ups that sound promising, hoping to reap some of those profits once the business is successful. Each of these is a way of investing funds in hopes that they will grow and provide you with an additional source of income, which you can use to secure your financial independence as an adult. This is known as *residual income* and is the money you receive when your investment has grown.

## WHAT TO EXPECT FROM THIS BOOK

Investing can be complicated, and you won't learn everything about it from this book. But this is a great way to start for those who want an introduction to investing and some suggestions for how to get started.

If you have studied economics or accounting, you may already be familiar with the basics of finance and investing. Many high schools now offer classes in life essentials that include how to balance your checking account, fix a flat tire and how to save for retirement (including saving and investing), among other valuable how-tos. Securing your financial future is a wise decision for people of any age. Learning how to wisely invest your money at a young age is one of the best decisions you can make for your future.

# PROFESSIONAL FINANCIAL ADVISORS

This book will provide you with a basic foundation to get started. But remember, investing can be a bad gamble if you're not prepared with the tools to make educated decisions with your income. Sometimes the best thing you can do is get the advice of a financial advisor, who can help you decide where and how to invest, what the tax issues might be, and how best to position yourself for retirement. Typically, these professionals initially assess your risk level to help gauge the best investment vehicles for you. Financial advisors make money either by a flat annual fee or by commissions from investment sales they make for you.

# THE IMPORTANCE OF EARLY INVESTING

Once you have a stable income, investing your extra funds is the best thing you can do for yourself. It is an effective means of putting your money to work and potentially building wealth. It may be possible to outpace inflation by investing smartly without losing ground to it if you invest intelligently.

Investing is more than just making money. This section reminds you why you're doing it. Don't forget to send it to that loved one who believes they're too young to start investing.

# Investing from a young age:

### 1. Enhances your ability to take risks.

In comparison to older generations who prefer safe and stable investments, younger investors tend to take on more risk.

Those who said risk equaled return weren't wrong when they said higher risk equaled higher reward. This is the sign you've been waiting for! Put your money where your mouth is (but make sure you do your due diligence first).

### 2. Compounding's potential

Putting your money to work to make you more money is the essence of compounding interest. When you invest your initial amount, you gain interest. This interest gets added to your invested amount, which increases it. By increasing the investment amount, the interest rate will increase even further. That would be great, wouldn't it?

### 3. Your financial habits will improve

Habits are diseases, as the saying goes. Great financial habits are definitely diseases on the positive side. When you start investing early, you will be able to make better financial decisions. It won't take you long to discover your money personality. Managing your money better, budgeting better, and living a healthy financial life will become second nature to you. If you invest your money early enough, you can never go wrong.

## 4. Secured future

Saving and investing early is the key to securing your future, and you might also be able to retire early if you do so. The need to borrow from friends or banks becomes lower and you'll be on the safer side if you do need money immediately for emergencies or unavoidable expenses.

When it comes to finances, investing early is probably the best decision you can make for yourself or your children if you plan on teaching them financial planning at an early age.

Don't wait any longer! Get started today! It is important to build wealth early in life in order to have a stable financial situation later on in life.

# CHAPTER ONE:
## TYPES OF ACCOUNTS

Having the right types of financial accounts, those that suit your business and financial purposes, really matters when it comes to investments. New investors are sometimes intimidated by all the types of accounts and investments available, but with the proper help you can start investing confidently. There are many online guides and resources that can help you to understand the basics of personal finance and investing, and you can meet with a professional financial consultant for more personalized advice as you're getting started.

In general, in order to begin investing, you will need at least an active checking account, which can hold and transfer your money as necessary. Setting up a savings account is also a terrific idea. This is where you keep a portion of your money set aside to be used as needed for larger purchases or in case of an emergency. When choosing a bank for your checking and savings accounts, pay attention to the perks they offer, including the interest rates they provide on your accounts. A high interest rate on your savings account equals more money in your pocket!

Your bank will also be able to advise you regarding retirement planning, college savings, and estate planning. Roth IRAs can help fund retirement, with tax-free contributions and no withdrawal penalties after a certain age. In this chapter, we will cover some of these accounts and how they benefit you as an investor.

## CHECKING ACCOUNTS

While checking accounts don't offer direct investment benefits such as stock management or significant amounts of accrued interest, they make investing seamless in other respects. A checking account maintains a record of all of your withdrawals and deposits, and usually allows for easy transfer of money to other accounts without additional fees. There are also brokerage checking accounts that make investing in stocks easier than with a traditional checking account.

In this section, we will cover traditional checking accounts and brokerage accounts, outlining the pros and cons of each while explaining the process of opening new accounts.

One of the main differences between a traditional checking account and a premium checking account is the interest that accrues and the requirements to keep these accounts open. With a traditional checking account, you get essential services for depositing and withdrawing money. Premium checking accounts may offer additional perks and interest rates, which you should consider when selecting your bank. We will cover the benefits of each account type, which can help you decide which one best suits your needs.

# TRADITIONAL CHECKING ACCOUNTS

These are typical benefits you might expect from a traditional checking account, but the details will vary by financial institution. Be sure to read the fine print and get all of your questions answered before opening an account.

## Benefits:

- Lower fees
- Lower minimum balance requirements
- Easy to open a new account

## Drawbacks:

- Higher fees
- Steeper penalties
- Typically have lower interest yields
- Lower withdrawal limits

## Opening an Account:

- Photo ID
- Proof of birthdate
- Social Security number
- Home address
- Phone number
- Minimum deposit requirement

# PREMIUM CHECKING ACCOUNT

Again, these are only the typical benefits you might expect from a premium checking account, but, as above, the details will vary by financial institution. Be sure to read the fine print and get all of your questions answered before opening an account.

Compared to a traditional checking account, premium accounts usually have the following features.

# Benefits

- Lower ATM fees
- Lower penalties
- Easy to open account
- Higher accrued interest with rewards programs
- Higher withdrawal limits

# Drawbacks

- Higher minimum balance requirement
- High minimum deposit required
- Monthly fee if minimum balance not met
- Not worth it if you don't make several transfers and use out-of- network ATMs

# Opening an Account:

- Valid photo ID
- Proof of birthdate
- Social Security number
- Home address
- Phone number

- Provide minimum deposit

# SAVINGS ACCOUNTS

Savings accounts offer a safe place to hold your money, and have other benefits beyond that. When you save money for investments, you want your money to build interest. Not only is interest important, but having an emergency fund for unexpected expenses is crucial. Many things can happen at a moment's notice and, if you aren't properly prepared, you may find yourself in debt faster than you can say millionaire.

When it comes to savings accounts, there are different kinds of accounts, each with different benefits. Those who only save money for a rainy day or perhaps a vacation will benefit from a high-yield savings account. Interest rates in this type of account fluctuate, and may not be good for long-term savings, as the yield changes frequently.

Those looking for savings accounts to grow income through future investments will need an account with liquid cash value and low fluctuation over time. This is a traditional savings account and differs in many ways from the high-yield savings account. Below the benefits of both types to help you decide which account is best for you.

# TRADITIONAL SAVINGS ACCOUNT

## Benefits:

- Money is insured
- Cash liquidity
- Balance doesn't fluctuate
- Use money from savings without penalties
- Easy access
- No annual deposit limits

## Drawbacks:

- Low interest yields
- No tax savings

## Opening an Account:

- Government issued photo ID
- Social Security number
- Proof of birthdate
- Address as listed on photo ID
- Contact information
- Link bank account info for deposits or transfers
- Initial deposit (typically $25-$100)

# HIGH YIELD
# SAVINGS ACCOUNT

## Benefits:

- Higher interest yield
- Easy transfers
- Daily compound interest
- Online management tools
- FDIC insured
- Easy to open account

## Drawbacks:

- More withdrawal limits
- Withdrawals require transfer to checking
- Long-term fluctuation of interest rates
- May require a separate bank

## Opening an Account:

- Complete the application at your chosen bank
- Provide personal information
- Provide a photo ID
- Verify identity
- Make initial deposit
- Name beneficiaries
- Set up online banking
- Link checking account for transfers

# CHAPTER TWO:

# HOW MUCH TO SAVE, INVEST, AND SPEND EACH MONTH

You may be thinking you don't make enough money to invest or save on a regular basis. However, don't forget that something is better than nothing. Saving just $5 a week adds up and makes a difference when it comes to investing and saving. Don't forget to invest in yourself by contributing regularly to a savings account. You won't ever be sorry that you have money tucked away to use when you need it.

If you work a typical part-time job making fifteen dollars an hour, you will bring home roughly $1,000 per month after taxes. Let's use this figure for our sample calculations, since it's a nice round number. A good rule of thumb to use for budgeting and saving is the 50/30/20 rule. This ensures you can pay bills, have some fun, and also put money away for savings. This rule allots 50% of monthly income to bills and other obligations, 20% of the remainder to savings, and the remaining 30% to use as you choose. If you find yourself strapped and unable to set aside funds for investing and saving, consider allocating ten percent to savings and ten percent for investing.

Investing and saving wisely are skills that can't be encouraged enough. They make the difference between having or lacking the funds for future expenditures and income to support you in your retirement. Many people don't properly manage their money and rarely save any of their earnings, much less invest them. In this chapter, we will discuss how much to save, how much to spend, and when to start investing whatever you can spare. We will also cover how to budget your income to be prepared for any scenario, including making sound, practical investments.

## LEARNING TO BUDGET

A budget is a tool for smart money management. For many people, however, it's also one of the more difficult bugaboos of adulthood. The difficulty with budgeting is not that it's hard to create a budget based on your income, rather it's difficult to hold yourself accountable to the budget you create and stand fast in the face of temptation.

As described above, the 50/20/30 budget breakdown is designed to guarantee money to cover bills, investments, and savings every month for the average household. The idea is that following this plan – fifty percent of monthly income is spent on household needs, thirty percent on wants, and twenty percent on savings – will ultimately lead to financial success. While this model is an excellent guideline, budgets should be specifically tailored for every individual or family. The most important idea is to make a budget and adjust it as necessary over time until you have a tool that works reliably for you every month, year in and year out.

Neither savings nor investing alone will make you rich fast. Every form of savings, from traditional accounts to IRAs, have the long term in mind, and your money needs to grow using the magic of compound interest to get you where you want to be in the future. That means no withdrawals unless absolutely necessary. Be aware that there could be a penalty when money is withdrawn. The penalty is typically ten percent but can be more.

Investing is not exactly like having a savings account. Some investments can make money for you in a matter of hours, but higher yield investments take time. The type of investments you make truly depend on the goal you would like to reach. Do you want to retire young or just earn extra income? How long are you willing to play the investment game and how much are you willing to risk? These are just a few of the questions you need to ask yourself before diving headfirst into the investment world.

# SPENDING YOUR INCOME

If you want to get technical, any time money leaves your possession for any reason, consider it spent. Many books and money gurus tell you how to spend your money and how to do it wisely. However, no one will tell you how to spend what you earn. The goal of this book is not to tell you how to spend your money, but simply to give you the tools and resources to make educated choices for yourself.

# EXTRA INCOME

Many people work full-time jobs to provide a living for their families, enjoy life during free time and vacations, and build a good retirement fund to provide for you when the time comes. Many of us start young in the long marathon that is the working world, but it's a marathon that you can win, rest assured.

We discussed saving, spending, and budgeting. You may be left with the nagging worry, "What if my full-time job isn't enough?" That is a question many people face today. With that said, today is a better time than ever to make extra income for better saving and investing. Here are a few ways to make extra income to pay off bills, save more money, and grow your investment strategies.

## Reselling

Yes, you can earn a full-time income by reselling items you purchase for cheap. At worst, though, you can make enough to cover a few extra bills you may have. In reselling, the goal is to buy a popular used item for cheap from a private seller, market, online site, or at places like Goodwill. You then clean or restore the item to better condition than when you bought it, and sell it for a higher price. Many people that have created wealth using this method, including the popular Gary Vaynerchuck.

Another option is buying pallets of merchandise that are either overstock or seconds. No improvement or cleanup work is required. You just post or advertise the items and make the sales.

## Food/Grocery Delivery

With the pandemic as part of our everyday lives, food delivery has become more popular than ever. Places like Uber Eats, DoorDash, Spark, Postmates, and others are busier than ever and always need new drivers. With the flexibility this gig offers, making a few deliveries every other day can bring in extra funds to stack your savings or investment accounts while still maintaining your full-time job.

## Lawncare

This side gig may require more work and more time, but with a used lawn mower in good working condition and a few overgrown lawns in need of care, you can easily earn some decent extra income in a single weekend. Depending on the area, you can earn upward of $25 per hour, which increases if you can secure several yards in the same general vicinity.

## Freelancing

The internet offers many opportunities to earn extra income. There are numerous tasks that can be done by almost anyone with a mouse and keyboard, as long as they know how to market themselves a bit. Here are a few types of gigs you can find on websites like Fiverr and Upwork where you can earn a little bit (or a lot) of extra income.

**Data Entry** - This is a gig nearly anyone can do as long as they follow instructions carefully and pay attention to detail. Gigs like these typically involve typing and organizing data on spreadsheets. There are countless jobs that offer $10/hour all the way up to $30/hour for skilled data entry specialists. Nevertheless, doing easy tasks like these for a few hours a week can be an extra $100-$400 per month depending on your ability and available time.

**Proofreading** - Proofreading is a high-demand job these days on freelance websites. Proofreaders are essential and needed everywhere for things such as articles, blogs, papers, research, and books like this one. Authors have limited time and deadlines to meet. In addition, it's notoriously difficult to catch one's own typing mistakes, especially if you're writing fast to get all your ideas on paper (so to speak). Sadly, too, many writers know what they want to say but don't necessarily know the right words to use. Proofreading jobs like this vary in pay, but are an excellent source of supplemental income and are generally sought for general proofreading, copyediting, line editing, and complex developmental editing.

**Virtual Assistant** - This position provides support to CEOs, managers, administrators, and busy executive staff who need assistance running their divisions and regional locations. Virtual assistants help with scheduling, customer service, appointments, data entry and data management, payroll, and other duties depending on the business. This job requires initiative, time management and follow-through skills, along with multitasking. If you have good organizational skills and enjoy interacting with others, this may be a great opportunity for you to make a difference and hone new skills for future advancement.

**Photoshopping** – If you know Adobe Photoshop, you have the skills to earn enough extra income editing photos. If you can alter photos to change lighting and backgrounds, remove unwanted pounds or scars, change hair color or even clothing (not to mention surprise photobombs), your skills may be in high demand. If you want to take this a step further, you can get certified in programs like Adobe Photoshop, leading to good gigs that pay well for cleaning up pictures for photographers and content creators.

In a perfect world, everyone would have well-paying jobs yielding enough income to spend, save, and invest. More often than not, that isn't the case. But if you make a point of saving *something,* it will help establish a habit of saving, and once that's in place you'll enjoy the feeling of knowing you have money in the bank. Put something away every payday and enjoy watching it grow.

# CHAPTER THREE:

# BEST SHORT-TERM INSVESTMENTS

Always do your research to give yourself the best possible advantage before diving into any financial matter. Understanding the basics of investing is a very smart move. Discussing your options with financial institutions and advisors is one of those smart moves that gives you options to make informed decisions.

## SAVINGS ACCOUNTS

As mentioned earlier, savings accounts are open accounts within a financial institution that allow you to make deposits directly or from your income source. Savings accounts do garner interest, but the amount varies. With this type of account, you will be limited on the number of withdrawals you can make every month.

# INTEREST

Money you earn from a financial institution by keeping your money in place for a required period of time is referred to as interest. This amount is paid directly into your account every quarter (three months).

## Compound Interest

Compound interest is interest paid on interest. The money you deposit in your account earns interest, which compounds (continues to grow) by earning interest on the interest paid every quarter. In other words, in an account that pays compound interest, the return is added to the original principal at the end of every compounding period. Every time interest is added to the account, your balance gets bigger. We will discuss this in much greater detail in Chapter 9

## Annual Percentage Yield

Annual percentage yield (APY for short), is the total amount of compound interest your account accrues per year. The total amount earned is calculated at your account's quarterly interest rate. It's best to have a saving account with a high annual percentage yield because your money grows faster.

Short-term investments are considered highly liquid, meaning you can access the money quickly with little to no penalty. Some people build their investment portfolios on short-term investments alone. However, short-term investments can be risky business. When you invest, your money is used by other businesses to help them grow, which in turn helps yet other businesses to grow successfully. It also means that you have less time to reap rewards like compound interest on the investment. Choosing a short-term investment also means you're limited in the investments you can participate in. There are eight types of short-term investments that have minimal risk and are highly liquid.

# EIGHT TYPES OF SHORT-TERM INVESTMENTS

# High-Yield Savings Accounts

A high-yield savings account is a federally insured savings product that earns rates higher than the national average. They earn around 1% APY. By comparison, the national savings average is 0.08% APY. Depending on the type of financial institution, you can open an account online or in person. You'll need to provide your Social Security number, contact information, and at least one form of photo identification, such as a driver's license or passport. (For a joint account, all parties must provide this information and ID.) You will be required to deposit money in the new account immediately. You can deposit cash, check, or make a wire transfer.

# Short-Term Corporate Bond Funds

A short-term bond fund invests in bonds with maturities of less than five years. Any entity can issue short-term debt, including governments, corporations, and companies rated below investment grade.

## Cash Management Accounts

This type of account is an alternative to traditional checking or savings accounts and is offered by brokerage firms. Customers can keep large sums of money securely and easily accessible while earning interest on the balance.

Every cash management account is unique, but you get easy access to your funds through a debit card and checkbook. These accounts typically sweep your cash into one or more accounts at program banks where your money is eligible for Federal Deposit Insurance Corporation (FDIC) insurance.

## Short-Term US Government Bonds

With short-term U.S. government bonds, you invest a specified amount of money in a larger fund contributed to by others. That pool of money is then invested in a government project or objective for a limited time. For example, the short-term bond may be for two years or five years. You earn money from this investment through interest deposits until the bond matures.

## No-Penalty Certificates of Deposit

A no-penalty certificate of deposit (CD), earns interest over a defined period, usually months or years. Unlike traditional CDs however, no-penalty CDs (also known as breakable or liquid CDs), allow early withdrawals without a penalty.

Treasury Bills (T-bills)

T-bills are a great short-term investment and often one of the safest investment options. Typically, you buy the bill from a government treasury at a discounted amount from the face value (i.e., you might pay $80 for a $100 T-bill). When it matures, you receive the bill's full face value, which is more than you paid for it originally. However, understand that the return is low compared to most other investments. When deciding if T-bills are a good investment for you, opportunity cost and risk should be considered. In general, T-bills may be a good investment for those who are nearing or at retirement.

## Money Market Mutual Funds

A money market mutual fund is a type of fixed income mutual fund that invests in debt securities characterized by short maturity and minimal credit risk. Money market mutual funds are among the lowest volatility investments. Income generated by a money market fund can be taxable or tax-exempt, depending on the securities the fund invests in.

## Money Market Accounts

A money market account is a savings account that generally earns a higher savings rate than traditional savings accounts. However, unlike traditional savings, you can only open an account with a hefty minimum deposit, typically $5,000 or more. However, if you are able to make that investment, you can enjoy the higher interest rate in return.

Money market accounts may offer some check-writing and debit card options. It's important to note that, alongside the higher savings return benefits of a money market account, certain restrictions may exist. Money market accounts often require that a higher minimum balance be maintained over traditional savings accounts.

## SUMMARY

When deciding whether short-term options work for you, consider all the factors at play, such as how soon you need the money, whether the type of investment has expensive transaction fees, and which type gives you the best compound interest.

No matter how you choose to invest your money in the short-term investment market, know that in general you are making a wise financial decision. Navigating such a market can make money, although it is certainly not a get-rich-quick strategy. There are ways to make money quickly that will be discussed in chapters to come, but as with anything, there are risks involved in such endeavors. Keep in mind that the accounts and options listed above are not for everyone. They are simply options you may want to consider at present or further along in your financial journey. Either way, equipping yourself with a solid understanding of what's available is always a smart move.

# CHAPTER FOUR:

# STOCKS & ALTERNATIVE INVESTMENTS

When you consider getting into investing, your first thought may automatically be the stock market. However, as with anything, the stock market has distinct advantages and also unique pitfalls. It's easy to get confusing information and make rash, uninformed decisions by jumping in too quickly. The stock market can change by the minute (literally), bringing you or costing you unpredictable amounts of money. It can also suddenly crash (a mass sell-off) based on world events, a new IPO (initial public offering by a corporation), or even a notable transaction by a celebrity, causing you to lose some or all of your money. Below are stock options that vary in risk and reward. As you go forth on your investing journey, consider all your options and consult a trusted financial advisor to ensure that you're making a reasonable decision that fits your financial goals and means.

Putting your money in the stock market is not a game by any means. It's like a contest of sorts, where the winner applies strategy, a lot of homework, accumulated knowledge, and sometimes pure luck. The more you follow and understand the stock market, the better your chances of building the fortune you're looking for.

Utilizing tools such as this book and other resources can help you close the knowledge gap between investing in stocks as a young investor and owning the savvy portfolio of your dreams. However, remember that it takes years of learning and practice to gain meaningful experience, but that doesn't mean you have to wait years to start investing. Sometimes it just takes some careful, responsible practice to learn the tricks of the trade.

There are numerous ways to get good basic investment information. You can start with books for a primary foundation, take a class at a community college, watch investment videos on YouTube, and/or join an investment group.

If you're looking for a starting point to gauge how much you already know about the market, visit the Financial Industry Regulatory Authority (FINRA) website. This organization regulates the brokerage industry. It's also an excellent way to test your investment and stock market knowledge to see how ready you are for buying and selling stocks (also known as "playing the market"). The website offers quizzes and scenario-based questions to determine how market-ready you are.

Beware of schemes and cons waiting to relieve you of your money, because, sadly, they're out there. Be cautious and don't hesitate to ask a reputable advisor if an investment opportunity you've heard about is legitimate or not. Arm yourself with the necessary knowledge to trade safely and stay abreast of new trends and opportunities. Like most of life, ongoing education is essential when it comes to investing.

Before you invest money in the stock market, the first thing to understand is the type of stock that's best for you to buy. There are fad companies that accept investment money, only for the business to fizzle out when the fad does. However, there are many established companies that have lasted through fads, recessions, and turbulence in the market or the economy in general. Those are the businesses to consider when choosing stocks to invest in. Finding a corporation with a strong track record and general principles you agree with, mixed with a reasonable stock price, is your first goal. The second key factor is how long you plan on holding on to the stock. Do you want to sell quickly or hold the stock for the long haul? Your investment goal and time frame will drive some of those decisions.

Before you begin to put your hard-earned money into the stock market, learn about the company you want to invest in, as you will literally become a stockholder in that company once you buy their stock. When you buy stock, you allow the company to use your money to fund the company's business, i.e., manufacturing gizmo widgets or refining crude oil. In return, you own a percentage of the company based on the amount of stock you own. Before choosing a company to invest in, carefully consider the following seven factors first.

# IS THE COMPANY GROWING BASED ON EARNINGS?

One of the primary things to look at when considering a company to invest your money in is the company's profit outlook. Is the business consistently showing a profit? If not, that is a red flag to pay close attention to. On the flip side of the coin, if you see a steady upward trend, that's an excellent sign that it might be a good business to invest in. To get a true understanding of business potential, look at its quarter financial reports as well as annual reports. Look for two or more years of consistent growth as a sign of financial and operational stability. Study the company's outlook, values, and long-term business plan. Does it have innovative ideas that will drive continued success with compelling products to draw in more customers and consequent revenue? Those are all good signs of a stable well-run company.

## COMPANY STRENGTH AND RESILIENCE COMPARED TO MAKET

Survival of the fittest is an operative principle in nearly every aspect of life, including the stock market. For investment purposes, choosing a company with strong industry presence is a smart move. Is the company you're looking at a leader in its field? You want to be sure that it's a solid competitive contender. It doesn't have to overshadow its competitors, but it does need to have a strong presence. Can it survive in a crowded market? Does it stand out? Don't hesitate to compare and contrast businesses to select those with solid standing. Look at their profit and stock performance over a span of two to five years.

# WHAT IS THE COMPANY'S DEBT STATUS?

Most companies are holding some form of debt. Many take out loans to get started and maintain a healthy debt-to-equity ratio to maintain their businesses. Even high earning corporations like Amazon and Apple have debt. Don't fault a business for the existence of debt, but be cautious of a high percentage of debt. If possible, find out the company's debt-to-equity ratio. This is a unit of measurement showing a company's market value alongside its total debt. To calculate this value, divide the total cost of liabilities listed on the published earnings statement by the total amount of shareholder equity. If the debt consistently overshadows the company's market value for more than a year in a row, that's an indication the company may have trouble managing financials and might not be a good investment. Savvy new investors focus on making low-risk investments. The debt-to-equity ratio should be 0.3 or less. Tech and construction companies typically garner more debt than other industries, because those industries rely heavily on debt funding. If a company is drowning in debt, however, it will push for profit, which will likely have a negative overall impact on its performance. If the debt-to-equity ratio is within acceptable norms, the company you're looking at could be a good investment.

## DECIDING VALUE BASED ON PRICE/EARNINGS RATIO

This should go without saying, but a company's price/earnings ratio is an important aspect to consider before you invest. The price/earnings ratio is also referred to as the P/E. This is a comparison measure that shows how well a stock is priced based on company earnings. When considering an investment company, the P/E ratio is a leading indicator of how fairly a stock is valued. To find this number, divide the company's share price by its annual earnings-per-share. Use the previous year's numbers, or those for the coming year.

Here's an example of how this would look in a real-world context. If a company stock trades at $40 per share and the earnings per share are $2.50 for the last year, the P/E ratio is 16. This is a below-average earnings ratio for a Fortune 500 company in today's market. Comparing companies by this indicator alone is a reliable method to weed out potential investment pitfalls. If a company has a lower P/E ratio, it will not be market valued as highly as one with a higher ratio. In some cases, the stock deserves a lower value rating; in other cases the market undervalues the stock, which may make it a good prospective pick. It's up to you to choose based on the information available to you.

## HOW A COMPANY TREATS DIVIDENDS

Dividends are excess profit a company distributes between shareholders. Typically, a company that pays dividends enjoys good financial standing and stability. This is especially true if a company pays dividends consistently at regular increased values. In some cases, you should be wary of frequent dividend payouts. When a company lacks consistency or has a sudden increase in dividend payouts, it could be a sign that it needs to attract or retain investors. This is particularly so if they have high yields and suddenly offer large dividends. High dividends can indicate that the company is not managing revenue well and that income isn't being invested back in the company. This doesn't fare well for stocks.

During difficult economic times, companies may temporarily or permanently change how they offer dividends to secure liquidity. This is not necessarily a bad sign. While it could depict trouble, more than likely the company needs access to cash to pay expenses. This may be a prevalent practice during times of inflation and other financial difficulties, such as a low earning year. Overall, look for breaks in patterns that don't match the current economic forecast or mimic what other businesses are doing. If a company chooses to cut dividends with no real explanation, it could indicate problems within the company.

## COMPANY LEADERSHIP

It's worth noting that a company is only as good as its leadership. If a company manages to succeed for a short period of time with an ineffective leader at the helm, their tenure may be short-term. Before deciding on a stock to invest in, it's worth looking into a company's leadership and using it as a measure to value potential stock. When considering what to look for in an effective leader, consider company culture, innovation, and flexibility. Also look for how much and how well a company invests in itself. Does it turn profit in order to increase its foothold in its respective industry? Well-managed companies tend to enjoy consistent stock increases, making them a stable choice for investment. Also check how long a leader has been in their position. A senior executive brings value to a company in both years and expertise. If you truly want to get a feel for a company's leader, oftentimes they upload speeches on the company website or other social media outlets.

## LONG-TERM STRENTH AND STABILITY

The stock market is volatile by nature. At some point, companies lose value in the market. What really matters, however, is long-term stability, which tends to occur over time. A company that weathers the vagaries of the market and doesn't have trouble when everyone else does due to economic factors could be a good investment bet. A stable company that grows revenue, maintains low debt levels, and is competitive with good leadership is probably a good bet. If one of these variables changes, investors should take note and determine whether it's a buy or a bust.

## ALTERNATE MARKETS

Alternate markets exclude stocks or bonds. While some investors put all their eggs in one basket, a wise investor knows to invest in a variety of ways in order to build a quality portfolio and gain the best advantage to earn substantial growth.

## Crowdfunding

Crowdfunding is a way to receive funding for a specific need or project and involves raising small amounts of money from a large group of people. Most crowdfunding takes place online on digital platforms.

## Equity Crowdfunding

Equity crowdfunding is a funding method used by up-and-coming companies that are new to the market. These companies usually have something new to the market and need help making their product visible. They use sources like Kickstarter to get their product and company going. When investing in companies on Kickstarter, you should verify the company's legitimacy and understand that they are looking for equity.

When you invest in startup companies, perform diligent research to learn as much as you can about the company's past and current status, as well at its future potential. Research future plans for potential products or services as part of its long-term strategy. Investments work best when there are known expectations over a specific period of time. If you've researched a company's products and services, you should feel more confident about your decision when it's time to make the initial investment.

## Real Estate Crowdfunding

Crowdfunding in real estate can be very lucrative if you pick the right properties and people to work with. There are ways to team up with people to make larger investments for more favorable properties. Some of these properties may need small repairs, but they are typically in high-demand locations that are expected to grow in the near future. There are websites similar to Kickstarter to find this type of real estate investment, such as Fundrise. As with any investment, make sure you do thorough research on the people you invest with and on each property you're considering for purchase.

## Commodities

Some investors like to invest in commodities such as gold, oil, gas, steel, wheat, and other items such as food, precious metals, or energy. Most physical items aren't practical to invest in due to the need for storage. This means that oil, gas, and food are not practical for most investors. The most practical long-term lucrative commodity option is gold and other precious metals. Silver can also fetch a good price if you buy and sell at the right times.

When it comes to investing in precious metals, you have a lot of options. Each metal has its own market and value, but diversifying your options can be very beneficial if you get them at the right price. Silver and gold come in the form of bars, bullion, coins, and different types of accessories like jewelry, pens, and watches. One of the drawbacks to owning physical commodities of this type is their storage requirements. For some investors, this can be a problem, especially in terms of security. If you buy silver and gold in bulk, there are ongoing storage and security issues. Since gold and silver are precious metals with high long-term value, you will incur the extra expense to secure and store them safely. As long as your budget allows it, physical commodities can be extremely lucrative for young investors.

When it comes to owning silver or gold, keep in mind that their value will fluctuate according to market demand. This commodity does well as a long-term investment for young investors. If you buy at the right time and carefully monitor the market, you should be able to make an appreciable profit. You can use those profits to broaden your investment portfolio in different areas you want to explore.

## Hedge Fund Investing

Hedge funds make large investments in stocks, but to help cushion losses, smart investments are made in securities as a counteraction. This mitigates large losses that could occur with large stock market investments. When you invest in a hedge fund, you pay annual fees that include a 2% management fee and the manager is entitled to 20% of the profits made from the investments.

It is also worth noting that not all hedge funds are the same. You can do extensive research to find a hedge fund that matches the criteria you are seeking. If you don't want to risk a lot, look for a hedge fund that allows a lower initial monetary investment. While many hedge funds can be on the riskier side of investments, there are also many conservative approach profiles available. If risk is your preference, then you should do your research and find the best fund that has a high risk-to-reward factor.

## Cryptocurrency

While this is seen as a newer type of investment, it has been around for a while. The market for crypto can be very volatile. Cryptocurrencies are created through blockchain technologies and data mining. Crypto is simply a digital currency. There are several different cryptocurrencies on the market and the most popular one to date is Bitcoin. This new currency type isn't widely accepted yet and cryptocurrency values are constantly fluctuating at present. A unique feature of Bitcoin and other cryptos is that you can produce your own. This is very unlikely for most investors, though, and is inadvisable. Data mining for Bitcoin is extremely time-consuming and requires massive amounts of equipment that is astronomically expensive. By the time you have invested in enough equipment to data mine one single bitcoin, you could already have invested in an entire real estate property and turned a tidy profit.

One of the biggest risk factors for cryptocurrency is the fact that it can be lost to hackers. Imagine investing thousands of dollars in Bitcoin just to have it all taken away from an unknown entity the next day. This is one of the factors currently contributing to the volatility of the crypto market price and values.

Cryptocurrency is still brand new and there is a lot of room for growth. The long-term value of cryptocurrency will undoubtedly increase dramatically, although the timing of this is uncertain. As time progresses and more countries around the world start developing regulations and methodologies for crypto, investors will start to see large returns on their initial investments.

# ARE ALTERNATIVE INVESTMENTS RIGHT FOR YOU?

As a young investor, you probably aren't ready for alternative investments, which often demand high income and require assets and net worth over one million dollars. For most young investors, this isn't an option until you have become well-established with a diverse investment portfolio.

This kind of investment requires a lot of capital up front, and can be difficult to trade both ways due to their illiquidity. However, if you're a younger investor in a position to afford alternative investments, then there are many approaches you can take, both risky and conservative. If you have the income, and stocks or ETFs are the types of investments you want to make, then alternative investments could be a great option for you.

# CHAPTER FIVE:

# REAL ESTATE INVESTMENTS

Real estate is by far one of the best alternative ways to invest. In today's society, owning a home can be a lucrative investment in a variety of ways. Some real estate investment options include renting homes, "flipping" houses, and utilizing your property as a short-term rental option, like AirBnb. In this chapter we will cover ways to turn home buying into a lucrative investment; moreover, we will teach you how to successfully use the same process repeatedly.

Real estate can be an easier way for a new or young investor to get a foot in the door by using leverage to invest. An investor can make a large down payment on real estate, which will allow them to pay the balance over time. This will allow you to invest in multiple properties or make various other investments to bulk up your investment portfolio.

An investor can take their investment a step further with each real estate property they invest in by taking out a second mortgage on their property. This gives them more money to invest in more properties they find, or they can use that money to make renovations on current properties they own to increase their value for resale.

# BEST WAYS TO INVEST IN REAL ESTATE

## Real Estate Investment Trusts (REITs)

REITs are a way to invest your money in the real estate industry without having to actually invest in a physical property. The best way to look at this type of real estate investment is to consider that you're investing in a company rather than a property. In this type of investment, you utilize a company that owns office buildings and rental properties. The best thing about REITs is that their dividend payout is substantial compared to other forms of investment. You can generate significant income this way or utilize the dividend payout to reinvest in more REITs.

# Building a Real Estate Platform Online

This type of investment venture can earn you fast, relatively easy money. However, the catch in this case is that you have to have money to make money. As with almost everything else, you can become a small-time investor on a website dedicated to helping people buy their first home, renovate, or even send a child to college. Connecting yourself with one of the online lenders allows you to have your investment paid back, plus some. These types of investments are considered liquid investments and can easily be unloaded if you no longer wish to continue investing that way. As stated earlier, though, in order to buy into the majority of lending companies you have to have an individual wealth of more than $200,000 a year or $300,000 for a married couple. You need amassed wealth of over a million to be accepted. This wealth status allows you to be accredited by the Securities and Exchange Commission. However, there are some online platforms that do not require such a steep monetary qualification.

## Invest in Rental Property

This type of investment can be extremely lucrative if you do your research. The ideal rental properties bring high rent value in high-demand areas. Typical areas include tourist locations, college areas, and locations near government facilities. Although these properties can be more expensive, you can typically bring in more rental income than the cost of your expenses, which allows you to pay the property off without using your own money. Rental properties can be even more lucrative if you buy properties that need to have work done. Bid low on the property, get a good price on renovations, and then get a new appraisal. After that, you will be able to charge higher rent if the property is in a favorable location.

## Consider Flipping Investment Properties

When you flip property, you take a risk at times, but the more experience you get doing this, the more your risk is mitigated. You buy a property that needs some renovations to make a profit on the equity in the home.

Sometimes even the smallest renovations increase a home's value by thousands of dollars. Once you start getting more experience, you will know what kind of repairs are manageable and more cost-effective to undertake. This will allow you to make investments that cost less and profit more. Just remember, if the property is in a high demand area, you will realize more profit. The sooner you sell the property, the less money you lose in mortgage payments. Your goal is to fix up the property as soon as possible to start marketing the property during renovations.

## Rent a Room

Renting a room may seem like an odd endeavor; however, when you consider the potential benefits not only for you, but also to a potential roommate, you may find it well worth looking into. While this is not necessarily a direct investment, it frees up money for investing and can be seen as a form of reinvesting in your home as it appreciates in value. Room rental can be a beneficial setup for the young, the old, and those in between. It can cut the cost of living in half. Considering how substantially rental prices for housing have gone up in the past five years, this can be a great alternative to save money and save renters undesirable fees and contracts.

If you do not feel comfortable adding a roommate to your mortgage or having someone live with you, all is not lost. You can still take advantage of this situation by utilizing your home as an Airbnb. This is a perfect option for those who desire to travel more but enjoy the stability of owning their own home. You can control how you rent your property, allowing tenants to stay either short-term or long-term. Also, Airbnb protects your home and its assets by guaranteeing protection against any damage.

Renting out a room may feel like a big decision and it may not be something you are interested in. However, it may be just what you're looking for. It may offer you just the right mix of freedom and manageability you need without the stress that other real estate investments offer. There isn't a right or wrong choice when it comes to real estate investment. The best choice is the one that benefits and serves you best. Whether you choose to have a hands-off approach with rental properties or you're ready to jump in feet first, it all depends on you and what works best for your lifestyle and availability.

# INVEST IN REAL ESTATE WITH LITTLE TO NO MONEY

## Buy a home as a primary residence.

Buying a home as a primary residence can be a way to get around strict lending rules. When it comes to investments, lenders consider them to be riskier and may not give you the money you need in order to invest. If they do lend you money, they will require a larger down payment, and possibly higher interest rates, which leaves less money in your pocket.

The only catch is that you will have to "live" in the property for at least one year before you can rent it out.

If you're willing to tough it out moving from property to property, you'll spend less money in the short-term.

Another benefit in doing this is a smaller down payment if you secure a VA or USDA loan. These loans aren't typically available for investment properties. If nothing else, this is another reason to move property to property. VA and USDA loans require little to no down payment at all, which leaves more money in your pocket to renovate or invest elsewhere.

## Buy a duplex — live in one unit while you rent the other one.

Buying a duplex can be a very lucrative ways to invest in real estate property. Investing this way allows you to pay most of the mortgage on the property with the rent you receive from the rental unit.

The goal is to live in one unit of the duplex while you rent the other unit. This is a very lucrative option due to the lack of investment you make. You spend less to pay off property that you own. Your lessee essentially pays most of the mortgage for you.

## Ask the seller to pay your closing costs.

Never be afraid to negotiate with a seller when it comes to closing costs. Many sellers are more than willing to pay closing costs as an incentive for a quick sale. In some cases, the seller will require you pay full asking price for the property. That is not always a bad thing, but if you choose to pay full price for the property, make sure you calculate a reasonable rent and make sure it covers your mortgage, insurance, potential repairs, and some residual left over for profit. If after all that, the total price of the property is more than you'd be willing to ask a renter to pay monthly, then you may need to negotiate a lower price and co-op with the sellers or move on to another property.

**Find a lender that pays closing costs or offers a rebate on your down payment.**

Lenders are often willing to help potential homebuyers with closing costs or offer incentive-based rebates on the down payment. Utilizing different lenders can save you a substantial amount of money, which can be used to reinvest in your home or another form of investment. Many lenders will prefer that lessees have a 680 or above credit score with a debt-to-income ratio of 45% or less. Quicken Loans and Freddie Mac are two great options to look into. Also consider using online platforms such as Rocket Loan for your mortgage.

# CHAPTER SIX:

## UNLIKELY WAYS
## TO EARN INCOME

In Chapter 2, we reviewed some common ways of generating extra income, especially through the gig economy. This chapter will be devoted to more ideas for generating income beyond your regular paycheck, which, if you have the time for it, can be a great way to boost your savings and investments.

## START A VENDING MACHINE BUSINESS

A great way to earn effortless income is by purchasing a vending machine. Passive income is easy to make because you earn without putting in a lot of your valuable time. Stock your machines by buying in bulk from a vendor and find safe locations with a lot of pedestrian traffic. Make regular checks on every machine to restock and collect the profits.

## RENT OUT YOUR CAR

If you find yourself in need of quick cash, renting your car to others is great way to do it. There are online companies that specialize in vehicle marketing in your area, and the car owner can often set the price. Make sure to do adequate research so you have appropriate insurance coverage for this purpose.

## WRAP YOUR CAR

If you don't mind driving a car covered with wrap or giant stickers, you can make money by advertising for companies. Companies exist that use vehicles as mobile ad machines and will wrap your car with ads. You can earn passive income up to $450 a month, depending on the ad.

## SELL STOCK PHOTOS

Anyone can sell stock photos with a little bit of practice. Today most people have phones with excellent cameras that can take beautiful pictures. Use your phone, along with some minor photoshopping and a little luck, and you might be able to sell your beautiful mountain, forest, and lake pictures on websites like Canva, Adobe

Stock, Envato, and many others. Prices for pictures vary, but the more your pictures are used, the more you sell. You can also create stock videos as well of wildlife, waterways, or even simple sounds of nature.

## PARTICIPATE IN SLEEP STUDIES

Sleeping is the ultimate way to earn passive income. You can literally make money while you sleep by signing up for various sleep studies. Sleep studies are used to advance knowledge about neural activity in the brain, and research companies and some universities pay to study your brain activity while you sleep.

During a sleep study, electrodes are attached to your head and you will be asked to sleep in different positions during the monitoring phase. What better way to sleep and get paid at the same time?

## RENT YOUR HOUSEHOLD ITEMS

Many people buy things they only use a few times before stowing them away. Why not rent them to people to make extra money? Think about that pressure washer you bought just to clean your siding or driveway. What is it doing now—sitting in your garage collecting dust? Most people need a pressure washer now and then, but don't need to buy one for a single use or two. Why not make money by leasing it out to people who need it once a year? Make sure you get business insurance when leasing household equipment. Ask your insurance broker for the correct damage, replacement, and liability coverage.

## RENT STORAGE SPACE IN YOUR HOME

If there's space in your home you aren't using, why not earn money by renting it to people who don't have enough storage space of their own? There are websites available to advertise that extra space, and you set your own price. This is a good solution if you live in a densely population area where housing costs are at a premium.

## RENT YOURSELF AS A LOCAL GUIDE

This one may not be for everyone, but if you know your local area well, serving as a local guide may allow you to earn money by sharing your knowledge with visitors. If you live in or near a tourist area and enjoy interacting with others, you can share local history and make recommendations for visiting nearby points of interest, popular shopping areas, and restaurants.

## HOST MEAL-SHARING EVENTS

Are you the locally renowned chef for your family and friends? Are you the go-to person when it comes to important holiday meals, celebrations, and special events? Why not earn money for something you like to do?

With the burgeoning population of getaway places like Airbnb, people want nice meals when they travel. You can deliver meals or invite people to dine with you at your own table. This could be a great option, especially if you're sociable and enjoy meeting new people. You can cater meals or events for friends and local businesses for meetings and conferences. Set a nice table or box up a gourmet meal and start advertising your host services! Bon appétit!

# CHAPTER SEVEN:

## CALCULATING ROI

# WHAT IS ROI?

Return on investment (ROI) is a common term in the investing world. Investments obviously cost money, and smart investors want to know just how much money their investments make for them. Your return on investment is how much money you make, relative to what you invested in the first place. For example, if you invest $100 and it grows over time to $125, then your ROI is $25. Investors consider ROI when deciding whether an investment is worthwhile.

ROI is also used to compare investments. Young investors typically have limited funds to invest and may only consider making a single low-risk investment at a time. They need to make every penny count or risk a negative return. That's why ROI is an important calculation. An investor takes the cost of each potential investment and decides which one will net the most money in their pocket.

ROI is also used in real estate investing. When a homeowner makes renovations, they calculate whether the renovation costs are justified. A homeowner may think it would be great to add a front porch to their home, but they also know they might move in a few years and the front porch project would be very expensive, up to $20,000. If adding that front porch will raise their property value and might allow them to sell their house for an extra $25,000 in the future, then building that porch is a worthwhile investment. It has an ROI of $5,000 (plus all those enjoyable afternoons sitting on the porch!).

However, if the porch would only enable them to sell the house for an extra $5,000 – because buyers don't really care whether there is a porch or not – then there is no ROI on the financial investment. The homeowner may still decide to build the porch, if those afternoons on a front porch would really improve their quality of life. But they would do so knowing there would be no financial ROI, and they might choose to invest their money in something else instead.

## HOW TO CALCULATE ROI

ROI is generally calculated using one of two methods.

## First method:

ROI = Cost of Investment ÷ Net Return on Investment × 100%

## Second method:

ROI = Cost of Investment ÷ (FVI - IVI) × 100% where FVI = Final value of investment and IVI=Initial value of investment

# INTERPRETING ROI

There are a few points to consider when interpreting ROI. While the simple examples we've used above – about building a porch, or investing $100 – have expressed ROI as a monetary amount ($5,000 and $25, respective), in fact, ROI is often expressed as a percentage. A positive or negative return on investment is the numerator in an ROI calculation.

An ROI calculation that yields a positive number indicates that net returns are positive, or "in the black," meaning they are above zero, because total returns exceed total costs. A negative ROI, on the other hand, indicates that total costs exceed total returns, resulting in a negative net return ("in the red"). It is important to consider annualized ROI with competing investments to make a fair apples-to-apples comparison.

It's relatively easy to calculate ROI for stock shares. However, it's more challenging when it comes to calculating the ROI of a business project, an undertaking that will probably require the services of an accountant.

# POSSIBLE PITFALLS WHEN INTERPRETING ROI

While the definition of ROI is fairly straightforward, and the calculations involved are generally manageable, it can still be difficult to interpret ROI accurately. It's one thing to determine a number, let's say 20% ROI. But it's quite another thing to know what that 20% is really telling you, and whether it should be considered a good outcome or a bad one. Below we'll discuss some of the pitfalls people face when attempting to interpret ROIs.

## Failure to Account for Holding Period

When calculating ROI, one disadvantage is that an investment's holding period is not taken into account, which can present a problem in comparing investment alternatives.

For example, consider investment X that generates a 25% ROI, whereas investment Y generates a 15% ROI. It's impossible to determine whether X is a superior investment without also knowing the time frame for each investment. If investment X generated a 25% ROI over five years, but investment Y generated a 15% ROI after only one year, it's possible that investment Y is actually the better choice. But we would need to know the length of time involved in order to make that determination. One way to do this is by calculating *annualized returns*; in other words, the ROI over the course of just one year. This allows us to better compare one ROI directly to another.

## No Risk Adjustment

Another disadvantage of ROI is that risk is not adjusted by ROI.

Risk and investment return are directly related: higher potential returns are associated with higher risk. Small-cap stocks tend to have higher returns than large-cap stocks, but they also have a significantly higher degree of risk, as is often seen in the stock market.

If an investor aims for a 12% portfolio return, for instance, he would need to assume a disproportionately higher degree of risk than someone who aims for a 4% return. It is possible for the eventual outcome to be very different from what was expected if the investor only considers the ROI number without examining associated risks.

## Omitted Costs

An ROI calculation that does not include all possible costs can lead to inflated ROI figures. An inadvertent or deliberate act can cause this result.

To calculate ROI for real estate, all related expenses must be taken into account. Interest on mortgages, property taxes, and insurance fall into this category, as well as maintenance costs, which are unpredictable since they also include other costs. The expected ROI can be reduced by these expenses. It's possible to overstate ROI if all costs are not included in the calculation.

# CHAPTER EIGHT:

# UNDERSTANDING CREDIT AND AVOIDING DEBT TRAPS

A solid credit rating can seem difficult to achieve, but establishing and building good credit is essential to long-term financial success. Those unfamiliar with the concept of credit may encounter a number of potential pitfalls. How credit works and how it can be used effectively are important concepts to understand.

Credit is essentially money loaned to you with the understanding that it will be paid back with interest. A student loan, a car loan, a credit card, and a mortgage are examples of credit.

## HOW THE CREDIT INDUSTRY BEGAN

Traditionally, borrowing money has been reserved for necessities like homes and farms, but in recent years it has become more prevalent. The Diner's Club card, introduced in 1949, was the first official introduction of consumer credit in the mid-twentieth century.

MasterCard and Visa were introduced just two years after Diner's Club. These lines of credit started slowly, and many people were hesitant to use them. However, over time, they have become widely used because of the freedom they provide to consumers.

The Visa and MasterCard logos are so familiar today it would be difficult to imagine life without them. The amount of debt we carry, along with our credit scores, are intrinsically linked to our consumer-centered society, where businesses and lenders place a great deal of trust on the consumer's ability to repay the debt they owe.

# THE MAJOR CREDIT BUREAUS

Before the introduction of credit cards, Equifax was the first credit bureau in the United States, established in the 1800s. Experian was formed in 1961, and TransUnion in 1968.

Currently, consumer reporting agencies are known legally as credit bureaus under the Fair Credit Reporting Act. There is no government involvement in these agencies. A credit reporting agency, PRBC, was formed in 2002 to allow consumers to build their own credit history by reporting bills that aren't typically included on credit reports, such as rent.

# CREDIT SCORE
# VS. BAD CREDIT

Your credit score is determined by analyzing your credit history to determine whether you are creditworthy; in other words, whether you are likely to pay back your debts on time. Your credit score is also known as. Your Fair Isaac Corporation (FICO) score. There are several common components in how this score is generated for an individual, though the exact formula can vary from one agency to another.

- Payment history: makes up 35% of your score
- Debt burden: 30%
- Length of credit history: 15%
- Types of credit used: 10%
- Recent credit searches and inquiries: 10%

The classic FICO score ranges from 300 to 850.

- A score of 300-599 is bad
- 600-649 is poor
- 650-699 is fair
- 700-749 is good
- 750-799 is very good
- 800-850 is excellent

# HOW DOES CREDIT WORK?

Consumers use credit to obtain goods and services immediately, with the understanding that they will pay for them later. Managing credit can be complicated, though, since you'll have to pay interest on the borrowed amount, as well as possible service fees in some cases.

Lenders will only allow you to borrow money if they believe you will be able to repay the loan. The process of establishing credit builds that trust. By borrowing and paying back money, you prove your creditworthiness and your ability to borrow in the future.

## YOUR CREDIT HISTORY, REPORT & SCORE

Credit reports are created by three independent credit bureaus – Experian, TransUnion, and Equifax – when lenders such as banks, credit unions, and credit card issuers report your borrowing and repayment history. An individual's credit report contains information about the number of credit accounts they have, their available borrowing limits, and the outstanding balances on each of those accounts. In addition, it includes records of any late or missed payments.

To determine your credit score, credit bureaus combine information about your credit history and current credit accounts to create a three-digit number between 300 and 850. An individual with a low credit score (closer to 300) is considered to have poor credit, while a high credit score (closer to 850) signifies good credit. The advantages of having a high credit score include better interest rates on mortgages and other types of loans, and higher credit card limits. When a creditor considers whether to extend you credit, they often review your credit score before making that decision.

Every year, you should check your credit report for errors. A free credit report is available to everyone every year. The annualcreditreport.com website or one of the major credit bureaus can provide you with a free annual copy of your credit report.

## HOW TO BUILD CREDIT

A person's credit score doesn't materialize overnight; it takes time and effort to build, which is why it's crucial to develop good spending habits as early as possible, in order to build good credit.

Good credit history and effective credit management give you a better chance of receiving a desirable credit card or loan. If you have never used credit, or if you have missed payments, you may have trouble getting approved for a loan or credit card. If you do get approved, you will likely pay a higher interest rate, which represents the risk the lender assumes.

Among the most common and effective methods for building credit for young people is using credit cards. Young people can learn responsible credit usage with credit cards by avoiding running up large bills and making all credit card payments on time. One of the fastest ways to damage your credit and wind up in debt is irresponsible credit card use.

There are other options for building credit besides credit cards. Making timely payments on student loans or a car loan is an excellent way to help you build credit. It is even possible to build a credit history by asking your landlord and utility company to report your on-time payments to the credit bureaus.

# WHY IS CREDIT SO CRUCIAL?

The purpose of credit scores is to determine whether a person is financially trustworthy or whether there is a high risk of default on their debts. A good credit score is essential if you want to borrow money for major purchases like a car or a house. Your credit score affects your ability to qualify for credit cards or bank loans for big ticket items.

Credit card companies and banks are not the only ones who use credit reports and credit scores. It is common for employers to check your credit report before hiring you. This tells a future employer how you handle financial responsibilities, which is an indication of your character. You may also be asked to provide a credit score when a landlord determines your ability to rent an apartment.

# CHAPTER NINE:

# MAKE SMART & LUCRATIVE INVESTMENTS

# HIGH COMPOUND INTEREST ACCOUNTS

Compound interest on investment accounts means that, in addition to daily interest on investments, you earn interest on your interest. We mentioned this briefly in Chapter 3 and will go into more detail here. It's clear that compound interest is a key concept in building wealth over the long term. Albert Einstein described compound interest as the eighth wonder of the world. Let's take a closer look at compound interest.

## Compound Interest Explained

Compounding is the tool that makes your investments grow each year. In addition to the earnings generated by investments, those earnings generate earnings of their own. There are mind-blowing possibilities in this relatively simple concept. You will see your investments grow faster if you allow them to accumulate compound interest.

If you invest $1,000 and it grows at 10% annually, then you will have:

| Elapsed Time | Portfolio Value | Gain in Five Years |
|---|---|---|
| 0 years | $1,000 | n/a |
| 5 years | $1,611 | $611 |
| 0 years | $2,594 | $983 |
| 15 years | $4,177 | $1,583 |
| 20 years | $6,728 | $2,551 |
| 25 years | $10,385 | $3,657 |
| 30 years | $17,449 | $7,064 |
| 40 years | $45,259 | $27,810 |

It's interesting to note that the modest $1,000 investment grew by $611 over the first five years. In the same time frame, that investment grew by tens of thousands of dollars without investing additional money.

Think about what would happen if you started with $5,000 or $10,000 and contributed money to your account regularly in addition to making smart investment choices.

# COMPOUND INTEREST VS. SIMPLE INTEREST

Simple interest is the interest rate multiplied by the investment (principal amount), as opposed to compound interest, which includes interest earned on interest already earned.

The term "simple interest" is commonly used in the context of loans or bonds where interest is computed at the same rate each period, without compounding. The term compound interest is often used in the context of investments and savings.

Interest can be calculated by the simple interest formula $A = P(1 + RT)$. Defining variables can be found in the following section. This means that the initial investment amount multiplied by one, along with the rate over time, equals the account value. Since the compounding factor is not included in the simple interest formula, it is simpler than the compound formula below.

# COMPOUND INTEREST FORMULA

Defining each of the variables in the compound interest formula will help us better understand the formula.

$P(1 + R/N)^{\wedge}(NT) = A$

**Principal:** P represents the investment or principal balance at the beginning of the investing process. Principal is also known as present value if you calculate interest using a spreadsheet or financial calculator.

**Rate:** The rate at which the investment earns interest.

**Number:** Calculates how many times interest is compounded per period. An example of an account that compounds interest monthly but has an annual interest rate is a savings account.

101

**Time periods:** T represents the number of periods.

**Account value:** The account value is calculated using the formula. The future value of this variable is also known as the future value of this variable.

In the case of $10,000 invested in a savings account offering 1% compound interest monthly, the interest would compound monthly. As a result of five years of savings, you would calculate the amount as follows:

$10,000(1+.01/12)^{(12*5)} = $10,512.49

# WHICH ACCOUNTS OFFER COMPOUND INTEREST?

When it comes to building wealth, compound interest offers several options. This investment strategy generates compound interest in the following ways:

**Savings accounts:** Banks lend you money in exchange for not withdrawing the funds from your savings account. A daily compounding savings account is the best since it increases your account balance more quickly than one compounded weekly or monthly. There are many local and online banks where you can open a savings account.

**Money market accounts:** Money market accounts are similar to savings accounts except they allow you to write checks and withdraw money from ATMs. A money market account usually pays a slightly higher interest rate than a savings account. There are downsides to money market accounts, such as monthly transaction limits and fees if your balance falls below a certain level.

**Zero-coupon bonds:** A zero-coupon bond generates interest equivalent to compound interest in order to compensate for the risk associated with owning a zero-coupon bond. No interest is paid to the holder of a zero-coupon bond, the bond is valued at face value when it becomes due, and the bond owner receives no interest payments (coupons) for holding the bond. During the term of the bond, the company may not be financially able to repay the full face value of the bond.

**Dividend stocks:** If dividends are reinvested, dividend stocks generate compound interest. All dividend payments you receive can be automatically reinvested and more shares purchased by your brokerage.

You are unlikely to find an account paying even 1% interest, despite the fact that both savings accounts and money market accounts are extremely safe. With different types of accounts and investments, you can significantly profit from compounding interest.

## Compound Interest is a Powerful Force

If you start investing early and remain invested over time, compounding interest can turn meager investments into wealth.

It takes time for interest to compound on interest, so if you invest early, you have more time to compound your interest. In the example above, a $1,000 investment grew by $983 in five years, then by $7,064 in ten years and $4,015 in thirty years. Your age at the end of 30 years will increase the longer you delay investing.

If you want to maximize the effects of compound interest, you need to stay invested. Your money can lose a lot of compounded interest if you constantly move or withdraw it whenever the market declines.

## Benefits of Compound Interest

The benefits of compound interest are shared by financial institutions and consumers alike. While lending the deposited funds to earn attractive interest streams, banks charge consumers compounding interest for not withdrawing money.

Over time, consumers can turn a relatively small nest egg into a healthy retirement account using compound interest either in the accounts described above or with stock returns.

# IRAS AND 401(K)S

While saving money for emergencies, vacations, and investments are all great ideas, it is worth noting that having a nest egg for retirement is just as important.

When planning for your retirement, you have two popular options: 401(k)s and Individual Retirement Accounts (IRAs). An IRA is an account that can be opened by anyone who meets the income requirements, whereas a 401(k) is an account sponsored by the employer or company.

The purpose of both a 401(k) and an IRA is the same, but there are some differences that make each attractive or unattractive to different types of investors. There are many differences between a 401(k) and an IRA regarding eligibility requirements, contribution limits, investment options, beneficiaries, and tax rules on distributions.

Retirement savings are made possible through employer-sponsored retirement plans such as 401(k). It is possible that your employer will match a percentage of your monthly contributions, which is free money for you. Conversely, you can open and maintain an IRA on your own and take advantage of its tax advantages and incentives.

Creating wealth through investing is smart and establishing a retirement fund early is just as important. The key to having a robust nest egg to retire on is letting the fund grow untouched. In other words, just let it be and don't spend it until retirement. It's tempting to dip into this fund when life throws you a curveball, as often happens (e.g., a new roof for your house), but resist that urge because unless you promptly pay the money back to your retirement fund, you may sorely regret the decision in your golden years.

## What is a 401(k)?

Tax-deferred retirement savings accounts, such as 401(k), allow you to save for retirement without paying taxes on your contributions. Retirement or early withdrawals from a 401(k) are when you pay taxes on the money. As a benefit to their employees, most companies offer 401(k) plans that permit them to defer their salaries for retirement. A portion of your monthly paycheck is automatically withheld and sent to your 401(k) plan before you receive it.

A 401(k) allows you to invest your retirement money either in mutual funds or exchange-traded funds. A plan sponsor selects these investment options to meet the financial goals and risk tolerances of employees. It is up to the employee whether they want to take a conservative or aggressive risk approach to their investments.

Many employers match employee contributions to their 401(k) plans as a way of encouraging participation. For employees contributing to their 401(k)s, the employer usually matches their contributions up to a certain percentage. The employer might match your contribution up to $2,100 a year if you earn $70,000 per year and the employer offers a 3% match.

Many people believe they know where all of their 401(k)s are, but only a small percentage of them actually do. 401(k)s worth $100 billion have been lost. Find yours!

# What is an IRA?

In simple terms, an IRA is an account that allows individuals to accumulate tax-deferred savings for their retirement. It can be held by a brokerage, a bank, or an investment firm. People can open an IRA account regardless of their employment status, unlike 401(k) plans that are restricted to employees of the companies that offer them. There are more investment options for IRA participants than for 401(k)s, and you can choose between stocks, certificates of deposit, real estate, index funds, exchange-traded funds, and more.

## IRAs can be classified into the following types:

**Traditional IRA:** Traditional IRAs are tax-deferred accounts, so contributions and returns are not taxed. Retirement money is only taxed if you withdraw it.

**Roth IRA:** Roth IRA contributions are taxed on deposit. Tax-free distributions will be made in retirement.

**Rollover IRA:** After changing jobs, you can transfer your 401(k) to an IRA. Since you are no longer able to contribute to the 401(k) plan of your former employer, this option allows you to keep more control over your investments.

**SEP IRA:** Employers offer SEP IRAs to their employees, and they are similar to 401(k). Unlike a Roth IRA, a SEP IRA allows contributions only from employers.

**SIMPLE IRA:** Employers can match up to 3% of employees' contributions, or make a non-elective contribution of 2% of salary.

## Roth IRA Account

Roth IRA accounts have set contribution limits that change from year to year, and the current year's limits are easy to look up online or inquire about with your bank. You can withdraw funds from a Roth IRA without penalty at age 59.5. The wonderful thing about this account is that withdrawals are tax-free not just for you, but for your beneficiaries as well, if you have named any.

Roth IRAs can be opened for children with a custodian to oversee them; there is no minimum age. Individuals have to be 18 or older to open their own individual retirement accounts.

## Benefits of a Roth IRA

- Tax-free withdrawals
- Tax-free growth
- Beneficiaries withdraw tax-free
- No withdrawal requirements
- Withdraw contributions anytime with no penalties
- No age limits
- Growth after retirement

## Drawbacks of a Roth IRA

- Taxed contributions
- Not included in employee retirement plans

- No rollover to traditional IRA
- Limited yearly contributions

## Traditional IRA Account

The biggest difference between traditional and Roth IRA accounts are taxes and withdrawal requirements. With a traditional IRA, you're taxed on your withdrawals during retirement just like you are for regular income, whereas contributions are tax-deductible and tax-free. The traditional account requires you to withdraw a minimum amount each year after age 71 (withdrawals must begin at age 72).

As with all accounts, Roth IRAs and traditional IRA accounts suit different people with different goals. In the following paragraphs we outline the details of each type of account. You can discuss these options with a financial advisor to determine what is best for you and your savings goals.

## Benefits of a Traditional IRA

- Tax deductible
- Compounding interest over time
- Can be converted to Roth IRA
- Full control
- Protected from bankruptcy/creditors
- Saver's tax credit

## Drawbacks of a Traditional IRA

- Contribution limits
- Income limits for tax deductions
- Required minimum distributions
- Early withdrawal penalties

Once you understand the different types of checking and savings accounts, you can decide which ones are best suited to your needs.

# DIFFERENCES BETWEEN A 401(K) AND IRA

Your savings goals can be met by choosing the right retirement account based on the differences between 401(k)s and IRAs.

As described above, here are the main ways that a 401(k) and an IRA differ:

## Eligibility

In order to participate in a 401(k) plan, you must be employed by an employer offering such a plan. Employees who wish to participate in the 401(k) plan may have to meet a certain age or service requirement.

An IRA is open to anyone who wants to join. Due to the fact that it is not employer-sponsored, any individual with an income can participate in the program and start saving for their future. The minimum contribution limit may be imposed by some institutions.

## Contribution Limits

In contrast to an IRA, a 401(k) has different contribution requirements each year. An IRA generally has lower contribution limits than a 401(k), and you can contribute up to $19,500 to a 401(k) in 2021. Plan participants over the age of 50 are permitted to make additional catch-up contributions of up to $6,500.

IRA contributions are capped at $6,000 for 2021. Those 50 years and older may contribute up to $1000 more as a catch-up contribution.

## Investment Options

The investment options available to participants in a 401(k) plan are determined by the employer or administrator of the plan. The most common investment options in a 401(k) plan are mutual funds or exchange-traded funds. There are several types of investments with different risk levels that participants can choose from, or they can spread out their retirement money across several types of investments. IRAs are alternative retirement accounts that allow you to invest in publicly traded stocks not included in the list of investment options.

A Roth IRA, on the other hand, gives participants the freedom to choose their preferred investments, without being limited to preselected investments selected by their employer. Investing your retirement savings can be as varied as buying stock in publicly traded companies, buying REITs, investing in index funds, buying bonds, and investing in certificates of deposit.

## Beneficiaries

401(k) plans automatically make one's spouse their beneficiary, who will benefit from the accumulated retirement savings upon the plan owner's death. It is necessary for the spouse to write a consent to the change if the plan owner would like to change the beneficiary. In the case of an unmarried person, naming a beneficiary is required.

In contrast, IRA beneficiaries can be named according to the participants' preferences. There is no requirement that spousal consent be obtained to change the beneficiary, and the beneficiary can be a spouse or anyone else.

## Distributions and Taxes

Roth 401(k)s and Roth IRAs are funded with pre-tax dollars, which means that the contributions are taxed at the time of contribution. It is tax-free to withdraw money from these retirement accounts. You are better off paying taxes now rather than worrying about taxes in retirement if you project that future distributions will push you into a higher tax bracket.

If you are 59 years old, you can start taking distributions from both retirement accounts ½. As soon as you reach 72, you need to start taking mandatory distributions and paying taxes on them. Before age 59, early withdrawals are allowed ½ taxes plus a 10% penalty tax are charged.

## Which Should You Pick?

It is important to choose the 401(k) or IRA that will help achieve your savings goals, since both have their benefits and drawbacks.

Your employer may offer a 401(k) plan, so you should enroll in it and start saving for retirement as soon as possible if you are eligible. Contributions to a 401(k) are higher than those to an IRA, and you can accumulate your savings over time. Because of the limited investment options, however, you cannot invest in a desired investment that is not among the available choices. You should consider taking up your employer's match if it is available and watch your investment grow.

Your old 401(k)s can be rolled over to an IRA if you would like to gain greater control over your retirement funds. Investments made through IRAs can be managed directly by the investor, and funds held in IRA savings accounts can be managed on a daily basis. You might also be able to take early withdrawals without paying the 10% penalty tax if you are buying your first home, paying medical bills, or paying higher education expenses. On the other hand, income taxes will still have to be paid on the withdrawal amount.

# WHEN TO STOP INVESTING

As a result of its numerous benefits, including increased income and greater financial control, investing has become a popular practice. Investment is a constantly evolving process, so most people are constantly preparing themselves to make the most of their money. You can make the right choice when you invest money by listening to your parents, trusted peers, and financial advisors. There are, however, very few investors who know when to stop investing. Once you have saved enough to achieve your goal without stopping, losses can be much more substantial than gains. Therefore, if you are confused and don't know when you should stop investing, this section will guide you through an assortment of situations when it would be better for you to make that choice.

One of the major elements of being a successful investor is knowing when to stop investing. Since investing is a long-term process, you must be cautious throughout your investment journey. You may find some of these scenarios concerning when to stop investing helpful if you are unsure.

## If You Have Crossed an Age Threshold

The age of the investor is one of the most important factors to consider when deciding to stop investing. Having reached a certain age, your priorities change and your goal may simply be a comfortable lifestyle. Over 50 years of age, you might want to stop investing in risky assets like stocks/equities, which are more volatile than other investments. Risky assets can be halted, but debt mutual funds such as Liquid Funds and ultra-short duration funds can be reinvested as they provide easy liquidity and are less volatile. Bonds, Treasury bills, government securities, corporate bonds, and other fixed-income instruments are all investments of debt funds. Investing in low-duration debt funds can earn you a steady income during retirement, particularly when you exit risky funds. Furthermore, liquid funds have higher returns than savings accounts. You can also make instant Redemption where the money can be withdrawn at any time.

## If Your Portfolio is No Longer Working for You

Investors who have invested for years would have encountered situations where their strategy did not perform as expected. It is possible that your approach isn't as effective as an alternative, or that your portfolio did not perform as expected. Getting out of the stock market is the right choice if you haven't made consistent profits in several years. When revising your strategy, many factors need to be taken into account. Have you invested in stocks before? What level of risk are you willing to accept?

With a new plan in hand, you will be able to move forward again once you answer these questions honestly. Therefore, it might be a good idea to stop investing for the time being and begin building a new portfolio instead. Ensure you focus on multiple assets when you re-start building your portfolio, such as mutual funds, ETFs, gold, and other diverse options, because multiple assets keep your portfolio balanced and strong. An ideal investment strategy would be to invest in one asset which does not always bring stable returns. The diversification of an investment portfolio balances risk and return, so if one asset in the portfolio gives a negative return, other assets in the portfolio can compensate.

## Experiencing a Dramatic Shift

An investor's ability to continue investing may be affected by changing circumstances in life. Take a loss of job, separation from your spouse, or medical emergency as an example: in general, your financial situation will change. It is possible that you will have to live temporarily on your emergency fund if this situation occurs. If that is the case, the most important thing for you to do is put back the money you have taken out of the emergency fund. After returning to work, you may wish to halt your investment until your emergency fund has been replenished.

## After a Certain Point, the Price Begins to Fall

A key aspect of investing in stocks is to buy at a low price and sell at a high price. As a stock's price increases, so does the risk investors take. You should remember, however, that there will always be a market decline. If you want to make good money off your investments, you must be able to determine the level of risk you can handle. A stock's past performance and trends are also important factors to consider. Observe what experts have to say and follow up with them. You should pause investing if they predict that the market won't get saturated soon and you will have financial troubles.

# In Case of Debt

A person's income is his or her greatest asset for creating wealth. A credit card debt, auto loan, or education loan that ensnares your most valuable asset for accumulating wealth is an indication of misery. You'll have more time to invest in your future if you pause long enough so you can break free from that chain. However, there is no need to worry. It is possible to start investing again as soon as you pay off your debt.

When people enter the debt cycle, it is usually because they took out a loan for a child's education, a wedding, or some other large expense, or they received cash during an emergency. Investing in advance and pre-planning your financial goals can prevent you from taking that route. You can invest your money for your future goals most effectively through a Systematic Investment Plan (SIP). In order to buy their dream house, a newlywed couple might start a systematic investment plan (SIP) to save for their child's future education. Taking this approach will help you avoid going into debt.

# WHEN INVESTING,
# CONSIDER THE FOLLOWING

It is recommended you sit down and take a closer look at everything after reading this book. You are still in charge of your own decision, as everyone's situation differs. You should consider the following factors before making your final investment decision.

## Financial Status

If you haven't made a financial plan before, sit down and assess your entire financial situation before making any investment decisions.

In order to invest successfully, you must determine your investment goals and risk tolerance – either independently or with the assistance of a financial professional. It is not guaranteed that your investments will yield a profit. With the right information about saving and investing and a well-thought-out plan, you should be able to gain financial security over the years and enjoy the rewards of management.

## Your Level of Risk Tolerance

There is some risk associated with every investment. It's important that you understand before you invest that you could lose some or all of your money if you purchase securities, such as stocks, bonds, or mutual funds. Your investments in securities are typically not insured by the federal government, unlike your deposits at a FDIC-insured bank or NCUA-insured credit union. In the event that you lose your principal, you could lose the amount you've invested. Investments purchased through a bank still carry this risk.

It is possible to earn a higher return on investment when you take on risk. Investing carefully in asset categories with greater risk, such as stocks or bonds, is likely to yield more money over a long term than limiting your investments to assets with less risk, such as cash equivalents. If you have short-term financial goals, however, you may benefit from investing solely in cash. Over time, inflation may outpace and erode returns on cash equivalents, which is the principal concern for individuals investing in cash equivalents.

## Variety Investing

When an investor includes asset categories with investment returns that fluctuate under varying market conditions within their portfolio, they help protect against significant losses. The returns of the three major asset categories – stocks, bonds, and cash – have not risen and fallen simultaneously historically. Asset categories that perform well in the market often suffer from poor or average returns in other asset categories. The overall return on your portfolio will be smoother if you invest in more than one asset category. By doing so, you'll reduce the risk that you'll lose money and reduce your portfolio's overall investment risk. You can offset your losses in one asset category with better investment returns in another asset category if one asset category's investment return falls.

Furthermore, asset allocation is crucial to meeting your financial goals since it determines whether you'll succeed. Your investments may not earn enough return if you do not include enough risk in your portfolio. The majority of financial experts agree that most portfolios should include at least some stock or stock mutual funds if you are saving for a long-term goal, such as retirement or college.

## Make Sure You Have an Emergency Fund

Investing wisely means saving enough to cover an emergency like sudden unemployment. It is common for people to save six months or more of their income, so they know it will be there for them in the future.

## Pay Off Credit Cards

You cannot find a more profitable investment strategy than paying off all your high interest debt. There is no strategy that can even come close. Under any market conditions, paying off your high interest credit card balance in full is the wisest thing you can do.

## Averaging Dollar Costs is a Good Idea

By adding new money to your investment over a long period of time, you can prevent the risk of investing all of your money at the wrong time with the investment strategy known as dollar cost averaging. Investing regularly with the same amount of money each time allows you to purchase more of an investment at low prices and less at high prices. The cost of averaging may be a good investment strategy for those who typically contribute to their individual retirement accounts at the end of the calendar year or early in April, especially in volatile markets.

## Rebalance Your Portfolio

A rebalancing is the process of returning your portfolio's asset allocation mix to its original composition. The goal of rebalancing is to ensure that you do not overemphasize one asset category or another, and to return your portfolio to an acceptable level of risk.

Your portfolio can be rebalanced either according to the calendar or according to your investments. Investors are advised to rebalance their portfolios every six or twelve months, according to many financial experts. Using the calendar as a reminder of when to rebalance is an advantage of this method. In the opinion of some experts, you should rebalance your portfolio only when the relative weight of an asset class rises or falls by a certain percentage. This method offers the advantage of letting your investments determine when you should rebalance. Rebalancing is most effective when done relatively infrequently in either case.

# CONCLUSION

There are wonderful investment opportunities for young adults just starting out. If you do a little homework about investing, talk to friends and trusted elders, join an investing group, start small, and save-save-save, you'll be well on your way.

The topics in this book will point you in the right direction, and there's a plethora of information online about any investing topic or term you could possibly think of. Start there and branch out.

When it comes to investing, time is on your side. The world is your oyster — start growing your pearl!

Made in the USA
Las Vegas, NV
19 December 2022

63594478R00079